Artificial Intelligence: Taking Over

How Will AI and Machine Learning Impact Your Life?

James Hendrickson

Table of Contents

Introduction

I want to thank you and congratulate you for purchasing the book, *"Artificial Intelligence: Taking Over - How Will AI and Machine Learning Impact Your Life?"*.

This book contains chapters that will help you get acquainted with the basic concepts related to artificial intelligence and machine learning, which are truly the next frontier in technology that can improve our future world. AI is an often misunderstood topic as people's knowledge of the topic is mostly influenced by films, television, literature, and even sensationalized news. So, it is important to have a solid grasp of what it is exactly and what it can do for mankind. Rather than perceive it as a threat to our current way of life, it should be regarded as an opportunity to advance the way we do things—by having machines that can do these things for us in brilliant ways that we were unable to imagine just a decades ago.

As in any other field of science, there are challenges that have to be overcome before perfecting a solution to a problem. These will also be discussed in this book along with the steps that are being taken to solve them so that AI will not negatively impact the lives of people around the world.

Chapter 1: History of Artificial Intelligence

Artificial Intelligence or AI can trace back its origins to ancient times when philosophers attempted to fit the idea of human thinking within a symbolic system. So, if man's rational thoughts could be as systematic as geometry or physics, then it can be mechanized. Even in antiquity, men were already bringing inanimate objects to life by designing clockwork automatons to perform simple tasks. Every great civilization in history has produced early precursors to humanoid robots. The earliest were religious statues found in ancient Greece and Egypt. These were believed to have been successfully given real emotions and minds inspired by the gods.

In the 17th century, scientists wanted to find out if reasoning could indeed be reduced to calculation. René Descartes, Thomas Hobbes, and Gottfried Wilhelm Leibniz all worked on the physical symbol system (PSS) hypothesis, the guiding philosophy of all AI research. PSS states that a symbol manipulation is necessary in reproducing human intelligence, so a machine can become intelligent just by encoding a symbol system into it. For example, the modern digital computer works on a system of symbols made up of ones and zeroes, also known as the binary system that allows it to perform processes that change its computer data. An artificial intelligence program is simply that—symbols expressing data that can be manipulated to perform processes. The main issue with this concept is that most people refuse to believe that their personhood could be reduced to calculations.

Breakthroughs in the field of mathematical logic in the 20th century inspired mathematicians to wonder if all reasoning can be formalized. The answers produced included the Turing machine. It was a hypothetical mechanical device that shuffled simple symbols like 1 and 0. Through this, it could imitate an infinite number of mathematical processes. This machine captured the essence of PSS and inspired scientists to explore the potential of thinking machines.

In 1950, Alan Turing, the father of AI and theoretical computer science, designed a test he named "The Imitation Game" that can test machine intelligence. This would later be known as the Turing Test. It involves a human judge trying to figure out if a subject talking to him through a computer screen is a machine or a human.

Later on, the term "artificial intelligence" was officially coined and defined in 1956 by Marvin Minsky and colleagues during a conference held at Dartmouth College. This landmark conference was attended by scientists who went on to become the proponents of important AI research programs. It was a historical event that gave birth to the field including its proper name, mission, and key founders. From then on, the future of creating artificially intelligent beings seemed bright.

However, interest in the technology and the accompanying funding for it dropped for a time until it was picked up again in the 1980s when Western governments decided to compete with the advancing efforts of Japanese scientists. Although, the 90s also saw the field being largely ignored in favor of personal computers, which had increasing demand in the market.

It is in 1991 when the Turing Test was first truly implemented via a contest. The annual event has yet to produce a winner that achieved the passing mark of answering 50% of the judge's questions successfully as specified by Turing in his original test.

At the turn of the 21st century, there was a boom in the market for AI products reaching a reported 8 billion dollars. Techniques in producing machine intelligence were being applied to solving a lot of everyday problems. The commercialization of AI has led to developments in tools and technology that will improve marketing, customer service, the Internet, medical services, transportation, consumer gadgets, and cloud computing among others.

Chapter 2: Philosophy of Artificial Intelligence

The philosophy of AI aims to answer the question: Is it possible to create a machine that is able to act intelligently? The answers of scientists differ depending on how they define "intelligence" and "machine." There are AI researchers who consider it enough for machines to be able to solve human problems using mechanized intelligence so that they simply simulate features of intelligence. For some psychologists and cognitive scientists, however, it is not enough for a machine to seem like it is thinking. To be considered as truly intelligent, it has to actually be thinking and have a complex mind that behaves the way a human brain does.

For Alan Turing, he defined intelligence simply as being able to sustain a conversation. As mentioned in the previous chapter, the Turing Test assumes that if a machine is able to answer questions in a convincing human-like manner, then it can be called intelligent. It does not test for human traits like kindness or the ability to be offended.

Hubert Dreyfus, Hans Moravac, and Ray Kurzwell all believed that if the nervous system follows laws of nature, then it can be reproduced as a physical device. Soon, computers will become powerful enough to simulate brain activity. This possibility has been predicted by scientists to be accomplished in as early as the year 2029. Even opponents of this theory believed that brain simulation is indeed possible. However, any processes done by a mechanized brain will only be mere computation and cannot truly mimic the human brain as a whole.

Computationalism, also known as computational theory of mind, posits that the brain and the mind is similar to a computer and a program (a procedure or algorithm). So if the brain is just a kind of computer, then computer can have both intelligence and consciousness—the two key issues that have to be addressed in designing AI. The physical symbol system hypothesis is a type of computationalism. At its core, the computational theory of mind claims that the mind is a symbolic operator with mental representations being symbolic representations. Complex mental states can be produced once the meanings of these basic symbols have been understood.

Another philosophical problem that faces AI scientists is machines having consciousness. Although some researchers do not find this issue very pressing, unless it can be proven that consciousness is needed for intelligence. Even for Turing, the more important concern is to first find out if machines can truly think. But for some researchers like Stan Franklin, Igor Aleksander, and Ron Sun, consciousness and intelligence go hand in hand. Once a machine becomes conscious, then it can be truly human. Others would refer to consciousness as having a soul. Thus, many wonder if consciousness is just the product of chemical and biological processes in the body, specifically the brain, or if it is from a higher plane of existence that only humans can ever possess. And if a machine is successfully imbued with consciousness in some way, then it could cease being a machine and be considered an authentic human being instead.

Along with the idea of machines having a soul, researchers are also looking into the possibility of machines having emotions. Because emotions and intelligent behavior are closely related, then perhaps it would be advantageous to have AI machines be capable of emotions. For some scientists, a good robot is one that has empathy, so the humans it interacts with would feel a kind of love. However, emotions can also be considered as a form survival instinct that dictates behavior towards what is good for one's species. An issue could arise when robots would feel more strongly about their own condition than that of humans.

This is connected to another problem in AI, which is the self-awareness of machines. Humans have what can be described as "free will." People are not told to think the way they do. They may have been conditioned by society and their environment to think and act a particular way, but for most people, they are in control of their thoughts. Because robots are created by humans to think a certain way, they are unable to think for themselves as they simply think in the way they are programmed. When a robot is able to break out of its programming, then it becomes human.

Another human characteristic that AI scientists are exploring in machines is their ability to be creative. Since computers can perform an astronomical number of processes (given enough storage capacity), then they might be able to come up with new ideas. Creativity is the driving force behind human progress. Machines might be capable of the same kind of progress at an even more exponential rate with their more advanced computing power.

That will bring about another very important issue in AI development, which is hostility or the capability of machines to become dangerous. Can a machine deliberately cause harm? This is a question of intention related to their supposed consciousness, which can also be closely linked to what they are feeling that made them turn hostile towards other beings. This valid problem is a concept that has been explored in science fiction. Futurists wonder if a scenario like this could be so widespread that it posed a threat to the existence of mankind.

Vernor Vinge imagined such a dystopian future where sentient machines have become more intelligent than men in an event he dubbed 'The Singularity." This concerns the belief in a technological singularity or the advent of a superintelligence that is forthcoming. Ray Kurzwell estimates that this could occur around the year 2045. It can have very positive effects on humanity, but when left unrestrained, it could lead to catastrophic results such as cybernetic revolt or AI takeover, computer virus epidemic, and a robot war.

These may all seem like fiction for now, but the acceleration of advances in technology in the recent years is evidence that they could be reality soon.

Thus, guided by the philosophy of Singularitarianism, efforts are being done to create "Friendly AI" or FAI where advances in the field are directed towards making AI humane and have a positive effect on humanity. This is largely concerned with machine ethics. Singularitarians are not opposed to the creation of artificial intelligence, but everything must be done prudently to avoid an AI revolution. The Singularity University, founded by Google, NASA and other technocapitalists, opened in 2009 to study and address issues facing the acceleration of technological change.

Chapter 3: What is Artificial Intelligence?

When regular people are asked to think of artificial intelligence, they would typically think of machine assistants that help around the house or robots that act like humans doing an assortment of odd jobs. However, when computer scientists are asked to define AI, they have a much more complex and different answer.

In the seminal text by Stuart Russell, professor of engineering at the University of California Berkeley, and and Peter Norvig, the director of research at Google, have identified four categories that AI can be classified into. These are: machines that are able to act like humans; machines that are able to think like humans; machines that are able to act rationally; machines that are able to think rationally.

There are subtle differences among these categories. For instance, a machine can be programmed to win at basketball, and thus, act rationally throughout a game as its aim is to win at the end. But, it does not necessarily think like a human being who is influenced by perhaps heckling by the audience, hostility from his opponents, or is able to strategize an idiosyncratic game plan with his teammates and coach. The machine simply does not process information the way a human basketball player does. Similarly, a machine that can think rationally based on computations and patterns will not be able to produce abstract works of art that a human artist as it simply lacks the imagination and out-of-the-box thinking that characterizes human thought.

A more concrete example is Siri, Apple's computerized assistant, which is a well-known model of AI. While it is able to act rationally by giving logical and sometimes playful answers to questions to the amusement of users, it merely responds to cues like keywords or the user's history and preferences. If it were to truly act like a human assistant, then it would have less of a robotic personality and give more inspired and less stilted answers. For instance, in conversation, humans interrupt the other speaker, pause and hesitate, use expressions like "uhm" or "oooh", and do not always speak in full sentences. Siri was not programmed to exhibit these more human traits, but there is a possibility of doing so for computerized assistants. However, perhaps a more flawed Siri is simply not as appealing and marketable to users. Giving it a more mischievous personality could result in inaccurate information. There is also the issue of safety. When using an iPhone's map navigation feature, it would be very dangerous to have an assistant that makes mistakes and gets lost—like a human navigator would.

There are also a lot of cognitive tasks that come easily and naturally for human beings, but would be extremely difficult for a program computer to do. For example, people do not have to think too much about seeing or interpreting non-verbal language. A computer is not able to easily process information that translates to a sense like vision or smell. This is the same when it comes to stimuli that can be interpreted as attraction or sympathy.

When it comes to computer vision, there have been significant developments in the field in the past few years. Machines that can see, which are essentially cameras, are now able to recognize facial features and interact with humans facing them. But, the technology is still far from completely reproducing the way humans see faces. Notions like seeing the "warmth in a person's eyes" or a fake smile are still incomprehensible to machines. Although, machines can now recognize 3D faces as opposed to simple 2D headshots of people. So, it no longer matters if a person has his head tilted to the side or wearing his hair differently. This is still far from perfecting computer vision. A major issue is that even cognitive scientist do not know exactly how facial recognition works in human beings, which makes it more challenging to mimic in machines.

There are some more tasks that are deemed by humans as "common sense" that machines find difficult to perform. For instance, a servant robot that has been programmed to serve food would be able to recognize an order and bring it out to the customer that asked for it. It might even be able to garnish it on the spot or serve a single portion from a larger dish. But, if a strand of hair that is completely visible to a human is found on the dish, the robot might still decide to serve it while a human waiter would know better than to do that as it is completely common sense. Human experience would dictate that seeing a strand of hair in food is not appealing as it is a sign of a lack of health and safety awareness in an establishment albeit hair in food will not automatically make people sick. Meanwhile, a robot could immediately dismiss it as harmless.

Unfortunately, "common sense" is quite hard to design. Computer scientists have come up with a few solutions to the problem but still face roadblocks along the way.

There is also the matter of learning. A concept close to AI research is machine learning, which is a kind of AI. However, there are pronounced differences between the two models, and this will be tackled in further detail in the next chapter.

Some machine learning is similar to the way human beings learn. A good example is Google Translate. The program uses statistical processes that evolve as more and more data is fed into the system. Humans do the same thing. They learn a language by looking at more texts or instances in verbal communication that inform the meanings of words and expressions. Language is acquired by examples. Nonetheless, Google Translate still makes mistakes because it does not yet fully understand different connotations or context of use. A human being can not only better pick up these language quirks, but he also has the added advantage of understanding tone of voice, accompanying gestures, and life experience to better learn a new language. With that being said, Google Translate is still a remarkable program as no person alive would be able to do such instantaneous translations in over 100 languages.

The great thing about AI is just the immense amount of work that it is able to do compared to a single human being or even a team of trained experts. That is why AI designers seem to be focusing on developing AI technology that is successful in doing very specific tasks within a limited context. As of now, AI machines are not expected to truly think and act like human beings do when faced with all different types of scenarios. Instead, they simply do what they are programmed to do and they do it very well.

Branches of AI

Given the vast number of applications for AI, the field has branched out into different specializations. More branches emerge every year and some are not yet fully defined, but these are the better established ones.

Logical AI

This involves representing the human world as a set of sentences in a logical mathematical language. This is what the program will use to decide the appropriate actions when faced with various scenarios so that it can achieve its goals. A number of concepts have arisen in logical AI such as common sense informatics situation and achieving human-level logic. It is easier to design formalized logic such as those used in physics and mathematics for AI than to program a machine to make decisions based on human-like reasoning.

Inference

While there are AI machines that were designed to perform mathematical logical deduction, they are still in a way limited because they are unable to infer based on facts. The addition of on-monotonic inference to logic has advanced the field of logic since the 1970s. It is grounded on the basic assertion that through reasoning, a conclusion, by default, can be inferred. But once information that is contrary to the conclusion is presented, then that conclusion becomes invalid.

An Inference Engine, while notoriously difficult to build, is able to better represent the world as it can express uncertainty in judgment and make judgments when data is missing.

Heuristics

A heuristic enables one to discover or learn an idea that is implanted within a program. It is closely related to the concept of "common sense" and could address AI issues that are associated with the development of common sense in machines. In current AI research, the technique is used to solve problem much more quickly than traditional methods. Speed is prioritized over accuracy, precision, completeness and optimization. Simply put, it is a shortcut. Forming an informed guess leads to a goal more readily in the hopes that the best possible answer can be obtained.

Genetic programming

Genetic programming is an approach that enables programs to find solutions to problems through a continuous improvement of a random population of programs. It is patterned after biological evolution where the selection of the fittest across generations will result in a well-adapted, well-bred population.

Common sense knowledge and reasoning

This branch of AI is the one that is very far from the level of human capability. Though, it is not for lack of trying as the area has been very active since the 1950s. However, advancements within this branch is still not enough to declare any major successes in the field. An important database that scientists have been relying on is the Cyc system, which is a compilation of common sense facts. While already sizable, the collection still needs to be refined.

Learning from experience

This method in AI development is called connectionism, which is closely related to neural nets. At present, programs are able to learn from experience. Although, they are able to only learn information or tasks that can be represented by their algorithms. This poses limitations to just how much a machine can learn.

Search

AI can sort through large amounts of data, which make them useful in search programs. Aside from its obvious use in search engines, AI can also take a look at endless possibilities such as different permutations of a solution or inferences for proving a theory. This can prove beneficial in a lot of industries.

Planning

Planning programs begin with facts like the effects of behavior in the real world and details about the situation at hand along with the goal of the program. Through these, they are able to generate strategies that will lead to the achievement of the goal. Essentially, it is a series of steps that will lead to the desired end result.

Pattern recognition

Patterns are recorded by a program and analyzed based on what it is programmed to do. AI that was designed for pattern recognition looks at patterns and tries to match it with what it knows. These could be natural language, game moves, statistical data, etc. More complex patterns involve more intensive algorithm than simple patterns.

Representation

In order for AI to understand the real world, it has to be represented in some form. The most common method is by using mathematical language. Other symbolic representations have also been developed throughout the years to serve different purposes and generate different meanings.

Ontology

Ontology is the study of kinds of objects. So in AI, programs are able to recognize what kind of thing is given its characteristics. This allows it to organize complex and vast amounts of information in a reliable and uniform manner. The field first emerged in the 1990s.

Chapter 4: Artificial Intelligence versus Machine Learning

When trying to understand artificial intelligence, it is important to differentiate it from machine learning. While the two concepts are closely related and the terms are used interchangeably, they are not the same thing.

The public may now be more familiar with the terms because of Facebook, Amazon, and Google that use the two types of technology in their products and services. They would claim that the use of AI and machine learning improves user experience, so most people have the idea that these concepts are helpful when integrated in daily life including gadgets, home appliances and other consumer products.

In that regard, artificial intelligence and machine learning are similar. However, in terms of definition, AI is a computer science that aims to create machines that are able to behave intelligently. On the other hand, machine learning is a science that is involved in getting computer to perform actions without need to be programmed to do them. Thus, while AI scientists are able to build smart machines on their own, it is machine learning that could possibly make them have human-like intelligence.

Nvidia and Google are two of the most active tech players working on advancing machine learning technology. They are focused on compelling computers to learn in the way that humans do so that they are able to think like humans. Scientists expect this to be the next breakthrough in technology as it will spark rapid advancements in many industries all over the world.

In recent years, it is machine learning that was able to offer the world different advancements in modern technology such as speech recognition, better web search, self-driving cars, fraud prevention, consumer behavior, image recognition, and a better understanding of human DNA. Because these programs learn from their experience, researchers are able to discover answers to questions in ways they were not able to do before.

Therefore, in order for AI to advance, machine learning must become even more reliable, efficient, and effective as soon as possible. That is how the two sciences are related to each other. Successes in one field will give birth to successes in the other field.

Unfortunately, the algorithms used in machine learning can still be further improved. That is why many of the major tech companies in the industry have it as one of their goals knowing that the next big innovation in the field will provide them with the foundation for new kinds of technology.

There are several types of machine learning. Each one differs in the way that the machine learns what to do when faced with a particular situation without explicitly being programmed to do so.

Reinforcement learning

This kind of machine learning focuses on how an AI machine is supposed to behave to fully optimize the work it does. So, that machine performs an action or a series of actions then gets a reward. It is akin to training a pet to perform tricks by giving it a treat after doing what it was told to do. This is also something that humans do. People like getting rewards for doing something successfully. They understand that failing to perform correctly will mean no reward, so they learn to do things properly in anticipation of receiving something positive in return in the form of perhaps a desired object, money or simple praise from another person. Machines can be programmed to "think" the same way. This is often seen in machines that are used to play games. Since they have to play to win, then they learn the right moves to become the winner and get the "prize" at the end. Although, it does take time to learn all the moves and become a complete expert in a particular task, which is exactly what professionals, athletes and artists have to do to be the best in their respective specializations or careers.

Supervised learning

This kind of machine learning involves having the researchers feed the correct answer to the machine. As with humans, they are able to learn information that they have been told to be true. It is a classic type of school learning where the teacher provides answers to the students so they could take their exams and pass the course. It is the same idea applied in machine supervised learning. For example, when shown a picture of a house, then the programmers give the answer "house" to facilitate learning how a house looks like. It is the most used method for training a lot of AI machines. Depending on how complex the task is and how large the answer database is, it can be very labor intensive and still not be accurate most of the time.

Scientists are working on refining the technology to be more reliable.

Unsupervised learning or predictive learning

Unsupervised learning is the most natural way to learn as it is instinctive. Like with humans and animals, they learn by observing the world around them and the other creatures that they interact with. When we were still very young, we quickly learned just by watching what our parents or siblings would do in a given situation. Even without anyone having to name objects and tell us explicitly what something is, one knows what they do and how one is supposed to act. Basic concepts like gravity is understood, even though a person might not yet been taught what it is called, what defines it and what its law is. People just know that dropped objects fall to the ground no matter what. Scientists are still baffled as to how machines can be made to perfectly think and act this way, especially at the same level that humans are able to.

Chapter 5: Practical Uses of AI and Impact on Human Life

Artificial intelligence has been applied in a variety of fields, although it is not always perceived to be AI because of how common it has become. AI has become part of larger technological systems since the late 90s to the present. It continues to be an important part of the infrastructure of many important global industries.

Computer Science

Computer science has long benefited from AI research to the point that many computer science technologies are no longer considered to be AI. Time sharing, user interfaces, interactive interpreters, the mouse, and storage management all began life in AI laboratories but are now ubiquitous in computer systems.

Finance

Financial institutions use artificial neural network systems that allow them to flag possible instances of fraud. The use of AI in the industry began in 1987 when Security Pacific National Bank used it in the prevention of unauthorized debit card use. Common banking applications like Moneystream, Kensho and Kasisito rely on AI as well.

AI is useful in operations, documentation, investment and property management, especially since it can react to changes even when businesses are closed and can better analyze market trends than humans.

Healthcare

In hospitals and other medical institutions, AI is being used in medical diagnosis, consultations, drug development and patient management. Doctors and technicians traditionally perform these tasks, but AI can help make more accurate decisions to further save lives. Many tech startups focus their efforts on creating AI technology for the Healthcare industry, because it is not only lucrative but will also have a tremendous impact in the improvement of human health including longer lifespans, the elimination of incurable diseases, and aid for high risk regions.

Heavy Industry

Jobs in Heavy industries are dangerous but necessary. Employees engaged in businesses involved in production, construction, mining, and the like are regularly threatened by hazardous working conditions. Robots can do these jobs and keep humans out of harm. Furthermore, many of these jobs are considered to be degrading and perilous resulting in a shortage of willing human laborers. The use of machines can address this labor shortage.

Customer Service

AI is currently being used in automated online assistants that are utilized on many e-commerce websites. The use of AI instead of human assistants is cost-effective as it reduces both training and operation expenses. Because of improvements in language processing, AI assistants are able to respond appropriately to customers in any language.

Several companies are working to improve customer service with AI. IPSoft is looking at emotional intelligence that will allow the AI assistant to empathize with the human customer. This includes the ability to adapt to different tones and word choices to better satisfy the customer's needs. Digital Genius is a startup that is looking at database of previous information from customer service interactions and using this to produce prompts that will help agents respond to problems more effectively. Inbenta's is looking at improving natural language so that the meaning of someone's words within a particular context is better understood.

News and Writing

AI can create analyses of reports and current news that will help professionals make quick and correct decisions. It can also sort through the billions of new information being generated on the web, especially on social media platforms, and predict trending news and even anticipate trends before they happen.

The technology can further be used to generate articles and content that have been optimized or even customized for particular readers, so that they respond well to the writing and enjoy the experience better.

There are also explorations in the use of AI to create literature with some being able to write stories and poems of true literary merit. By understanding what readers like, AI can generate excellent literature that humans will respond well to.

Aviation

Airplane simulators that run on AI are used to train both commercial and combat pilots. Because AI can simulate the behavior of other human pilots and air traffic controllers, pilots will learn to anticipate the problems that they may face in a real life scenario without risk to their own lives.

NASA is also developing AI software that allows aircrafts to repair damage to itself without the need for human agents. This is especially crucial in high-risk environments like outer space that are dangerous or impractical for humans.

Transportation

The use of AI in transportation will lead to safer and more reliable transportation that also reduces its impact on human communities and the natural environment. AI can change the way people are able to move around from self-driven cars and anti-drunk driving mechanisms to controlling traffic and bus and subway timings. Aside from commuting, transportation is also an integral part of many business processes. Being able to transport goods faster and more efficiently can lower overhead costs and provide products to end consumers faster.

Music

Musical compositions can also be done by AI with virtual composers being developed to score movies or compose pop hits. AI can be used to study sounds and music that are popular or elicit desired reactions from audiences. It can then use this information to generate its own unique musical compositions. The medical field will also benefit from AI-generated music as it can be used in therapy for pain or stress-relief.

Gaming

AI is being developed for use in video games where humans can play against video game robots. Playing against a computer is not a new concept, but an AI machine opponent will not only be smarter but also be more entertaining and encourage deeper emotional investment in human players. There are also AI toys that have autonomy and can serve as pets or even playmates. They can serve an educational purpose for children, too, by introducing them to important digital and personal concepts in controlled and programmable environments.

Chapter 6: Challenges Present in AI Research

In the next few years, AI research has the goal of making sure that the technology's impact on society is beneficial and stimulates research in the fields discussed in the previous chapter. Scientists working on AI have to be extra mindful of how their innovations could affect individuals. For instance, when a personal computer crashes, it might be annoying for the user, but in most cases, it is not completely devastating. However, if a machine that runs on AI like a self-piloting airplane or a robot medical assistant makes a miscalculation or misses, the result cannot be considered as a minor glitch or setback that people can easily recover from. Especially since AI is being used in already inherently dangerous fields like the military, weapons manufacturing, and law enforcement, the risk of misapplication and abuse increases. Any destructive or scandalous event that can be attributed to AI will only hinder progress in the field and cause fear in the public. Thus, funding and support for AI research will weaken as private companies and government sectors will refuse to invest in something that has already been proven to backfire.

One of the priorities in the long term is the achievement of "strong AI" or true as defined by John Searle in his Chinese room hypothesis. Rather than simply simulating a human mind as in what is called as "weak AI" the computer actually is a mind. When this succeeds, then machines will be far superior to humans in terms of performing cognitive tasks. Consequently, computer intellect will advance beyond human intellect and this could be harmful to mankind.

However, it is also possible that by developing super-intelligence, man would be able to create technologies that will help eradicate poverty, disease and war, thereby ushering in a new age of peace and human evolution. The birth of strong AI could be the most important event in history, but it could also be the final event that will lead to man's demise.

There are many people who doubt the possibility of creating a strong AI, while there are others who do believe in the possibility and that its existence will be advantageous to humans. Many also recognize the possibility of a super-intelligent being to cause harm to humans, whether deliberate or not. As such, the research being done today should focus on preventing such negative consequences from ever happening by developing AI with goals that are aligned to the goals of humans. In the end, mankind will be able to maximize the full potential of AI without suffering any untoward results.

Many scientists have come to the conclusion that a super-intelligent AI will be human-like in a sense that it has feelings like hate or love. So, the program will not deliberately be malevolent or benevolent. Instead, if AI were to indeed become harmful, then there are two likely situations.

An example of AI systems that were designed to hurt human beings are automated weapons. When operated by a hostile party, these weapons can kill a lot of people. Furthermore, the arms race can result in mass killings sparking devastating wars. And because part of the efficiency of AI weapons is their ability to be difficult to control by opposing forces, even their original controllers might lose power over them as they act of their own accord. This is already true of early AI technology—sometimes the machine does its job so well to the disadvantage of the user. The negative effects could, then, be tenfold when dealing with inherently dangerous and more intelligent AI technology.

Thus, even if the AI was created for a good intention, it formulates a harmful method to reach its ultimate goal, especially when its own goals are not completely aligned with the user's goals. For instance, when a self-driven car is set to bring a passenger to a particular destination in the shortest time possible, it might take dangerous shortcuts and hurt people along the way to fulfill its duty. Technically, the automated car did its job well and efficiently to the loss of humans around it. On a larger scale, an AI technology designed to improve the environment by eliminating harmful pollutants might decide that it is best to target the source of the pollutants like factories and other enterprises that produce waste. In the same vein, humans will also be perceived as a threat and the ultimate source of these pollutants. By eliminating humans, the environment will truly be free of pollution.

So, it is not about creating machines that might turn out to be malevolent. The problem is that these machines might become too competent. What is important for AI research now is to ensure the safety of humans in a world that is improved by super-intelligent AI. Important personalities in like Elon Musk, Bill Gates, Steve Wozniak and Stephen Hawking have all already voices out their concern in the media with regard the risks of super-intelligent AI. Thus, the public is also a lot more aware of the challenges facing AI research.

Although, the success in the creation of strong AI will catapult humanity into a new age, and day by day, progress in the field is being made to achieve that aim. Experts predict that super-intelligence will be created within this lifetime with researchers setting the date by the year 2060. However, if the goal is to create safe AI, then it might still take centuries to get to that point.

As AI could potentially become more intelligent than humans, then it might be difficult for human scientists to comprehend how they will behave. Hence, man has not yet invented solutions to problems that they might pose and none of the technology that already exists today could defeat them. An extraordinary consequence of this, though, is that humans might have to drastically evolve again in order to defeat super-intelligent AI. When taking a look at evolutionary history, homo sapiens always evolved in response to threats in its environment—climate change, dangerous predators, disease. Humans might have to adapt once more to the threats posed by AI. Some of these threats will be discussed in the next chapter.

Chapter 7: Threats of AI to Human Society

As AI and machine learning develop in ways that exceed the capabilities of human thought, they will be able to perform more and more complicated tasks that humans were not built for. It makes sense that the idea of super-intelligent robots frightens people because their existence means that humanity loses its superiority in the world. And so, it would be good to consider the downsides of the advancement of AI.

First, as outlined in the previous chapter, a threat that looms over any research that seeks the formation of super-intelligent AI is that they may become malevolent. It seems that the best way to combat this AI threat is to not create AI machines that have goals of their own—easier said than done, but with care, it is possible. Like personal computers and gadgets being used today that are capable of doing tasks that the average person cannot, it should not be problem to develop technology that is infinitely more intelligent than humans, especially when these machines were built to serve humans.

Unfortunately, man does make mistakes and there is always the possibility of a scientist creating, whether intentionally or not, an AI that seeks itself and has its own motivations. One way to curb this is to create an AI police that regulates and catches AI before they turn malevolent or before an innately dangerous AI does damage. This is similar to how laws and security have changed over the past few years in response to more technologically advanced crime. Of course, AI will also advance cybercrime the way that information technology over the years has spawned new types of crime or new ways of committing traditional crime. Digital identity theft, online scams, spread of prohibited materials and hacking are "new" computer-based crime that did not exist before. So it is not difficult to imagine that there are individuals and groups that would look towards committing AI crime that will affect society. Once the technology is out there, it will become possible to appropriate AI technology that were initially created to do good things to instead commit crime.

Another threat of hyper-capable AI machines is the replacement of human labor. This already happens with every technological revolution. The creation of steam-powered machines replaced manual workers and improvements in manufacturing plants usually mean laying off many factory employees. Because machines can do work faster, more accurately, and without human weaknesses like fatigue or stress, many companies will opt to upgrade to AI systems. Thus, skilled laborers will no longer be in demand. However, when certain types of jobs become outdated, new types of jobs are also formed. Before, computer engineers, web analysts, social media marketers, app developers and tech brokers were not careers. But now, many companies have job opportunities for this kind of talent. Even businesses that are not in the IT industry still have departments dedicated to IT or have IT jobs integrated into their traditional business systems. Nonetheless, rapid acceleration in the replacement of traditional jobs by AI machines might indeed have devastating effects. It will take a long time for humans to develop skills and educational programs that will continue to make them relevant in a world run by AI, while AI will continue learning and improving—humans might just not be able to catch up. Also, the generation of workers that will suddenly find themselves out of a job could create an economic problem and contribute to widespread poverty.

Traditionally secure and high-paying jobs like that of doctors, engineers and lawyers could be obsolete in just a few months and be replaced by machines that cost less and make fewer life-threatening mistakes. Regular jobs like waiters, drivers and cleaners that employ the majority of the population will now be made available to computers that are sophisticated and gets the job done more smartly. Moreover, when people do not have jobs, they will not have enough income to support these new AI-improved businesses. Thus, regardless of the efforts to cut costs and optimize processes by businesses, they will still lose business because the rest of society can no longer afford the products and services that they offer. A more extreme outcome is that society could descend into anarchy and chaos in a bid to survive in a world that deems them as dispensable.

For Stephen Hawking, Elon Musk and other computer scientists, the biggest threat that AI poses to humanity is existential in nature. Simply put, humans will now be at risk of extinction. The enemy here will be the element of surprise. Humans will be unable to predict the moment when machines become superhuman as they will no longer depend on humans to tell them what to do and how to behave. This is because they will no longer think in a predictable way that humans can anticipate. The result could be a global catastrophe that will swiftly hit the world and that humans can no longer recover from.

Even putting safeguards or "kill switches" on AI machines could prove to be useless as the computers learn to outsmart their built-in limitations. Sentient computers can also band with others to greatly increase their potential. In addition, many scientists believe that computers cannot be imbued with some sort of morality. Intelligence, even among human beings, is different from moral wisdom. Human morality is thought to be innate, perhaps a gift from the divine. Those who are less spiritual may argue that morality is conditioned by society. AI machines might be able to grasp the concept of morality but, in the end, find it still find it "smarter" to forego what they perceive to be human weakness in the pursuit of their own goals. It is ridiculous to expect machines to be bound by ethical rules especially when they were not programmed to have principles and values aligned with that of humans.

The AI machines that do achieve a level of emotional intelligence might also see themselves as human. This type of anthropomorphism is a concept that is widely explored in literature with many influenced by the theme of Pinocchio: Is a robot boy a real boy? As such, should they be treated as humans and be afforded the same privileges that humans have? The employment of robot servants could now be regarded as slavery, and could result in robots fighting for their own rights to freedom. These freedoms could include wages, the right to have families, and access to resources. Anthropomorphic behavior also includes the ability to deceive, lie and cheat humans as people do with one another.

The development of super-intelligent AI will lead to the creation of a new race of beings. Social issues that used to divide humans in terms of class, religion and ethnicity will now also divide humans and robots. Traditional social structures might need to be changed to accommodate AI citizens. Humans might find themselves to be the minority or underprivileged class as opposed to super-intelligent machines. If this were to happen, it would be reasonable to assume that humans will also try to fight back and perhaps even to their demise.

Ultimately, this notion relies on the idea that robots crave power in a way that humans do. They might not want power but still work towards it as a means to their goals. Such a speculative sci-fi plot might seem too insane to be possible, but that is also what earlier ancestors thought of telephones and cars. Even today, there are still people who do not believe in Google Glass, self-driven Uber cars and Amazon drone deliveries. Those who do believe in these new types of technology might perceive them as dangerous and will refuse to patronize these products even when they are already made available to the mass consumer market.

The fear of AI machines will always be there, and perhaps that is for the best. When people are wary of and careful about the AI technology being created, then more systems will be put in place to guard the integrity of these AI machines. Although, another reaction could also happen, which is to simply abandon AI research entirely for fear of the harm it could do to humans. That will not be beneficial to humanity in the end. Instead, it is important to make a conscious effort to plan for the future of AI in a way that controls all the threats that it poses.

Conclusion

Thank you again for purchasing this book!

I hope this book was able to help you have a better appreciation for what artificial intelligence and machine learning means, and what innovations in the field can do for the future of mankind. Indeed, once you have better understood a concept, it is no longer something to be frightened of. So, imagining robots taking over the world and machines plotting against humans should be regarded as sci-fi fancy as actual scientists do work hard to avoid having the technology backfire on us.

Furthermore, I hope that you also see the world in a different light and can now recognize the importance of AI in products and services that you use every day from doing simple web searches to living in smart homes. It is an incredible innovation and the forthcoming AI revolution should be an exciting event to witness in our time.

Finally, if you enjoyed this book, then I'd like to ask you for a favor, would you be kind enough to leave a review for this book on Amazon? It'd be greatly appreciated!

www.ingramcontent.com/pod-product-compliance
Lightning Source LLC
LaVergne TN
LVHW052126070326
832902LV00038B/3961